# ON SOCIAL MOBILITY

# ON SOCIAL MOBILITY

## A BRIEF HISTORY OF FIRST GENERATION COLLEGE STUDENTS@MICHIGAN: 2007 TO 2019

## DWIGHT LANG

Maize Books

Ann Arbor, MI

Published in the United States of America by
Michigan Publishing
Manufactured in the United States of America

DOI: dx.doi.org/10.3998/mpub.11460152

ISBN 978-1-60785-519-4 (paper)
ISBN 978-1-60785-520-0 (e-book)
ISBN 978-1-60785-561-3 (open access)

*Front cover photo:* This September 2017 photo was taken during the first meeting of First Generation College Students@Michigan at the new first generation center: First Generation Student Gateway.

An imprint of Michigan Publishing, Maize Books serves the publishing needs of the University of Michigan community by making high-quality scholarship widely available in print and online. It represents a new model for authors seeking to share their work within and beyond the academy, offering streamlined selection, production, and distribution processes. Maize Books is intended as a complement to more formal modes of publication in a wide range of disciplinary areas.

http://www.maizebooks.org

*Encounter the Other*
*Interrogate the Familiar*
*Understand the Self*

For all the First-gens

# Contents

# Acknowledgments

I would like to thank Rob Sellers (Vice Provost for Equity and Inclusion and Chief Diversity Officer), Karin Martin (Professor and Department of Sociology Chair), Angela Dillard (Associate Dean for Undergraduate Education, College of Literature, Science, and the Arts), and Fabian Pfeffer (Associate Professor, Department of Sociology) for their support regarding the production of this book. Jason Colman (Director, Michigan Publishing Services) consistently encouraged this project and Amanda Karby (Senior Digital Publishing Coordinator, Michigan Publishing Services) coordinated critical details of publication. My wife, Sylvia Wanner Lang, has been a constant companion, especially recently as I recalled important first-generation events of the last twelve years.

I am grateful to countless individuals—especially Greg Merritt, Elise Bodei, Dilip Das, and all Michigan students (both undergraduate and graduate)—who have been invaluable champions of and contributors to First-Generation College Students@Michigan over these many years. First-generation developments of the last twelve years remain great sources of fulfillment and I am gratified by the opportunity to have been part of important institutional changes at the University of Michigan.

I

# INTRODUCTION

———

W hen we reflect on the establishment and growth of any organization or collective effort on a university campus, we must acknowledge numerous contributions over time. The University of Michigan undergraduate group First-Generation College Students@Michigan has benefited from countless efforts of many individuals who sought to recognize and raise awareness of students who are first in their families to attend or graduate from college here in Ann Arbor. This brief history identifies those who effectively contributed to these worthy efforts.

In 2008, many Michigan first-gens began to openly recognize their challenging experiences and this became a welcoming invitation for others to speak up. By revealing their vulnerability, students acted with courage and generosity. What had been kept

———

quiet inside became the basis of connection and community, and slowly, but surely, a public story emerged: stories about invisible students at Michigan; stories that made the invisible visible; a thoughtful movement that was hard to ignore. There is always power in shared determination.

I cannot tell every story about this grassroots initiative and there are many more stories that could be told—of that, I am certain. And although it is impossible to thank everyone who kindly gave their time and energy to this project, I'm sure those who read this history will recognize themselves on the book's pages and in the photos that document various stages of development. I especially want to acknowledge all first-gen students—both undergraduate and graduate—who stepped up year after year and who continue to carry forward the first-gen banner that keeps our movement alive. I hope this book generates fond memories, inspires others to continue contributing to first-gen initiatives here at Michigan, and provides perspective on how institutions of higher education change when challenged to do so.

Aside from individual efforts, I would also like to recognize important institutional forces that helped create, sustain, and grow First Generation College Students@Michigan. A number of university administrators played vital roles in cultivating our first-gen group, certainly the first undergraduate group of this type at Michigan and possibly the first one in the nation when it was established in 2008. I've identified departments and offices (including individuals) that very early on and over-time recognized the necessity and logic of supporting this important, too often ignored undergraduate and graduate population. (See Howard Kimeldorf's essay in Chapter 3.) All of you have our sincerest appreciation. Various media sources also played crucial roles in raising awareness of Michigan's first-gen experiences. (See various published essays and programs starting in 2009 cited later in the book.) I thank numerous individuals who willingly wrote stories or supported the writing of stories highlighting first generation student perspectives and deeply held emotions.

As we recognize first-gen student experiences in the twenty-first century, I also reflect on the early seventeenth century in northwestern Europe and England, when new social class systems of capitalism chaotically emerged and were eventually exported worldwide, including to the British colonies of North America. These class systems evolved and shaped life outcomes of millions down through the centuries. Today, Michigan students—whether working-class, middle or upper-middle class, or even very wealthy—continue to be defined by social classes they're randomly born into. America's complex class system also impacts the educational institutions we create and sustain. Colleges and universities, including Michigan, will hopefully provide assistance to students born into various socioeconomic circumstances and help them better understand those who are different as well as the history of social class structure in the United States, its current manifestations, and how and why it continues to matter.

# Social Stigma, Institutional Challenges, and Changes: 2007–2019

As faculty adviser to First-Generation College Students@Michigan over the last twelve years—and as a first-generation student myself—I've had opportunities to witness significant institutional changes. Social class diversity is now publicly recognized at the University of Michigan. Fortunately, class differences on Ann Arbor's campus are no longer ignored and unspoken or considered too controversial. (See Chyrisha Brown's essay that provides insights about typical first-gen experiences and emotions prior to 2008.) For this I am grateful. No longer does the university fear stigmatizing students from lower income families by openly identifying their presence. (See Elise Bodie's essay.) No longer is the university anxious about being stigmatized by peer institutions for acknowledging that too many students from lower income families are in attendance. (See http://americantalentinitiative.org.)

Michigan now readily admits that social class inequality is experienced by students from all racial and ethnic groups. This is an important change and has multiple effects on campus culture. There is increasing recognition that social class distinctions students bring to campus persist and manifest themselves—not always visibly—within various campus settings. This helps challenge long established social stigmas associated with working and lower class lives in America. As a result class stigma no longer silences Michigan first-gens from the outside and shame no longer silences them from the inside. There's no need to hide and feel unworthy. First-gens need not have blurred self-images because their presence goes unnoticed. No longer is it overtly stated or implied that where low income students grow up is less than or nothing when compared with students from more privileged families. All student voices are encouraged and have value. And we now have our long-awaited first-generation student center that recognizes the complexities of social class differences: Michigan's First-Generation Student Gateway. Imagine that!

Low income first-gens will likely continue struggling with tough questions of how they will inevitably return to their homes and communities as different people, with new, college-acquired middle-class values, ideas, language, and behaviors. Many still worry: "Can you ever really go back?" They'll continue thinking about whether they can successfully assimilate into a middle-class campus culture or anticipated middle-class lives, careers, and communities, and wondering what it would be like to potentially marry a person born into economic privilege and someday raise middle-class or upper-middle-class children. Nowadays, however, Michigan offers more support to first-gens: acknowledging their presence and important contributions to the university; celebrating their unique social class backgrounds and cultures; helping them thrive, not merely survive; and assisting them with inevitable and difficult decisions associated with upward mobility.

But one might also ask: Why did some students and the University of Michigan become more aware of these social class issues starting around 2007? Was this only related to the emergence of First Generation College Students@Michigan? Or were other factors at work?

My own view of this heightened awareness of class developed after the passage in the fall of 2006 of the state-wide Proposal

2—Michigan Civil Rights Initiative—a successful ballot measure eliminating race- and gender-based affirmative action in college admissions throughout the state. After Proposal 2, the University of Michigan understandably became concerned with (1) how to maintain various types of desirable social diversity; and (2) how social stratification extends beyond racial differences.

I watched campus debates regarding affirmative action influence student culture in dramatic ways. Many students wanted the university to continue with race-based affirmative action, while others were happy to see the end of this admissions policy. Some asked why seventy-five percent or more of underrepresented minorities at the university (African Americans and Latinx) grew up in the middle and upper middle classes. Why weren't there more talented underrepresented minority undergraduates from poor and working-class backgrounds? Why weren't there more talented white, Asian, and Native American undergraduates on campus from lower-income households? And why wasn't affirmative action also social class–based? Unsurprisingly, debates were intense and filled with emotion. Local and national media carefully followed policy discussions and inevitable differences of opinion. The University of Michigan's race-based affirmative action policies even made their way to the Supreme Court.

Fortunately, students started thinking more deeply about the complexity of diversity and stratification in higher education and around the country. Many felt diversity wasn't just about race. Michigan's low income, first-gen undergraduates—regardless of race—started seeing themselves in new ways in relation to the ninety percent of undergraduates, both students of color and white students, who grew up in varying degrees of affluence. They started thinking more about economic inequalities pervading

American society and how these inequalities manifest themselves on college campuses. This created, I believe, an environment where many first-gens became much more aware of their distinctive status at Michigan. The university's politically complicated setting and changing culture also encouraged a new willingness to talk more openly about social class differences, first-gen lives, and how these conditions influence individual experiences.

# Recognition, the Problem with No Name, and Institutional Prestige

While witnessing first-gens talk about their Michigan experiences, I've also thought about thousands of first-generation students over the decades who felt invisible here in Ann Arbor. Not being publicly recognized by the university prevented first-gens from becoming fully self-conscious—to achieve the autonomy they needed to transform themselves and start their journey toward upward mobility. Sadly, they may not have been able to discuss the challenges of social class transformation with anyone at the university. (See Chyrisha Brown's essay.) This mysterious first-gen "problem with no name" was a daily certainty students coped with privately because the institution did very little to publicly or internally highlight the myriad social class backgrounds its students represented. This, unfortunately, led to a type of institutional classism that left first-gens with little or no support and painted the small number of first-gens as necessary but not preferred Michigan students. As the university was discreet and seemingly ashamed of its first-gen students, it stigmatized them, while indirectly promoting shame, silence, and confusion around students trying to find their way.

A vital part of this classism was and is how the American Dream is normally interpreted in higher education. First-gens have been and still are routinely informed that anything is possible if they simply work hard and achieve. Those with social class privilege like this message because it reinforces their faith in and experiences with middle-class, meritocratic excursions in higher education. First-gens too often hear that they should be eager to move beyond the economic circumstances they were born into and overcome whatever deficiencies they might have; that they ought to leave behind their working-class identity and proudly become middle class—a better class—because America would celebrate their victories over economic disadvantage, even if these students had to alienate most of their family members in the process; that they will be better than or several steps above communities that carefully raised and watched over them. But to say "you'll be better" is carelessly elitist and cruelly reinforces routine public shaming of poor and working-class Americans.

Another insidious part of American and institutional classism appears as first-gens begin upward mobility journeys on campuses like Michigan's. The portal to the middle class that college provides is framed with judgments and expectations that subtly humiliate students as well as their families, friends and neighbors. First-gens easily read between the lines: you come from those people who failed to achieve middle-class success—the American Dream—and now you should be appreciative for getting this chance to attend Michigan.

But as they encounter this "problem with no name"—a problem that's often hard to verbalize once they recognize it—first-gens can never forget the challenging economic circumstances where their families remain. They return home for holidays and summer breaks, finding themselves between their new world and the world where they were raised. They are liminal and often feel detached from both. Sometimes they send money home each month after working late in dormitory kitchens, dining rooms, libraries, and ground crews. Unfortunately, Michigan and other selective colleges have failed to recognize or haven't carefully thought through powerful, invisible, social class struggles persisting at the individual level. But social class lingers everywhere on campus, even after graduation. Historically, first-gens have found it hard to openly talk about their struggles to achieve upward mobility and the feeling that they couldn't be their authentic selves in Michigan's pervasive and idealized middle-class campus culture.

As you read various descriptions and accounts in this book, you'll recognize the considerable difficulties faced by first-gens over the decades who silently strolled down campus sidewalks, thinking about how they were changing deep inside. As faculty adviser to First-Generation College Students@Michigan, I've heard countless passionate stories from students over the past twelve years. While eating lunch in dormitory cafeterias or sitting in classrooms, students wondered if they might ever be able to safely disclose complexities of their social class heritage. Would they ever meet first-gen peers or understanding staff members with similar first-gen backgrounds? Some connected with other first-gens by chance at games in the Big House or the Crisler Center, attending various campus events on the Diag, taking breaks between classes, or perhaps enrolling in a course from that rare self-identifying first-gen graduate student instructor or professor. But would they ever really fit in?

Before the 2006 Michigan Civil Rights Initiative, the university likely feared any open acknowledgment of social class diversity would imply declining institutional prestige—especially if too many working- and lower-class students attended Michigan. Now these students are openly hailed and efforts to enroll even more students from lower-income families contribute to the university's status. For example, since 2016 Michigan has been part of the American Talent Initiative, a coalition comprising 290 of the nation's highest-ranked colleges and universities that seeks to enroll an additional 50,000 high-achieving low-income students in coming years. In addition, Michigan recently made public its Go Blue Guarantee (https://goblueguarantee.umich.edu/), which offers free tuition to admitted undergraduates whose parents have assets below $50,000 and earn under $65,000 per year. This tuition program and developing changes in campus culture tell America that the University of Michigan is now concerned with intrusive social class inequality, and that it seeks fundamental human dignity for all students. The Go Blue Guarantee also increases public recognition of Michigan's leadership role in higher education. Institutional prestige has been and continues to be an important consideration here in Ann Arbor. In 2019, admitting more talented students—who have grown up in economic disadvantage—has fortunately become part of a larger public quest for the common good. One cannot help but think that honest and determined first-gen storytelling in previous years helped change how Michigan and other universities address social class inequality.

# Risk Takers, Boundary Crossers, and Social Class Immigrants

I know that first-generation students are talented risk takers and boundary crossers: they're intelligent and resourceful social class immigrants. I've witnessed these courageous tendencies in action during the last twelve years. First-gens willingly take risks and cross socially constructed class boundaries to attend colleges with long-term, majority, middle, upper middle, even upper class traditions and enrollments. These journeys routinely happen around the country, especially at more selective colleges and universities like Michigan.

When upward social mobility does occur in America it is normally a multi-year process. Starting in one's 20's or 30's, for example, some individuals born to the working or lower classes—who do not attend college—might work their way up America's social class hierarchy, eventually landing in the middle class. For lower income, first-gen students at Michigan, however, the early phases of upward mobility are packed into four short years. Instead of gradually assimilating into middle class culture over a ten to twenty year period these students are suddenly introduced into social spaces they have little or no knowledge of. Most first-gens are usually up to the challenge.

As I've thought about and observed their risk-taking, I think first-gens are likely experiencing something similar to what Germans call "fernweh:" a word meaning "far-sickness" or wanderlust—a desire to travel to distant places. First-gens want to be somewhere different from where they were raised, but are simultaneously worried about what might become of them once they arrive. Will they change in unexpected ways during the immigration process? They're pushed and pulled by profound desires to remain close to home and family but also drawn by mysterious social forces toward unknown, distant places inhabited by people with different histories, stories, behaviors, and attitudes.

First-gens literally leap into the unknown when starting at colleges like Michigan—physically, emotionally, and intellectually. They're in classrooms where middle-, upper-middle-, and upper-class students are in the majority. These peers grew up in wealthier secluded suburbs; place high value on individualism and competition; and have likely traveled numerous times to locations outside the United States before high school graduation. This new place—and its unusual inhabitants—is very different from their families and communities that stress group needs over individual aspirations. Still, this self-imposed separation from home quietly encourages and even compels explorations of sought-after, profoundly different social worlds—far, far from home. First-gens are tested by an unfamiliar academic world with new ways of thinking, talking, and acting. Should they quickly retreat to the safety of the familiar? Should they embrace this alien yet attractive environment? Can they effectively cope with the internal turmoil? Unfortunately, universities have not always recognized these social class questions and experiences.

As this mysterious "fernweh" washes over them, I've seen Michigan first-gens not only challenging and changing themselves but also transforming this university. I've observed their impact on decision makers, faculty, and fellow students who have grown up and continue to live in economic privilege. By openly talking about the realities of social class difference and carefully reflecting on pervasive conditions of inequality, they're also changing the national landscape.

First-generation students have always made significant contributions to our campus culture, but they can now do so publicly, proudly acknowledging their important histories and class cultures. This creates a healthier campus climate for everyone—students with more modest class backgrounds, students who grew up in the middle and upper middle classes, and students born into significant wealth. Low-income first-gens can now be authentic rather than silently feeling like imposters, ashamed by the fact they were born and raised in poverty or in the working class. They no longer need to keep secret that their parents didn't attend college or wonder why it's so important in Michigan's dominant middle-class culture to keep this information out of sight and mind. Now the "problem with no name" is finally named and spoken about here in Ann Arbor.

But an unanswered question remains: Why did all these changes take so long to emerge? This brief history might help provide some needed answers.

This book and the various media stories cited within not only recognize considerable first-gen student accomplishments but also identify multiple strengths first-gens will proudly carry into their twenty-first-century endeavors. Pride in one's social class heritage and a willingness to talk openly about social class differences in America are clearly reflected in our first-gen motto: "We may be the first, but we won't be the last."

# 2

# WINTER SEMESTER 2007

Chyrisha Brown ('09) and Associate Director of University Housing Greg Merritt discover that a first-gen undergraduate group has never formed at Michigan. They wonder why. Greg encourages Chyrisha to start such a group. Greg and Undergraduate Adviser in Sociology Elise Bodei (Frankish) also discuss the possible development of a first-gen group. See later essays by Chyrisha Brown (Rucker), Elise Bodei (Frankish), and Greg Merritt regarding anticipated and unexpected challenges and concerns.

3

2007–2008

---

## Fall

Greg Merritt and Elise Bodei initiate a meeting in Palmers Commons for interested U of M staff to discuss first-gen experiences. Topics include: How do first-gens negotiate this side of their identities? Why does the university not publicly acknowledge the presence of all first-gens? Why isn't first-gen status identified in student records? Some staff members say they wouldn't ask students about being first-gen because this might make advisees feel embarrassed, offended, or both: embarrass first-gens by calling attention to the fact that their families are low income and different, or offend students from higher-income families by assuming they might be working class or living in poverty.

So how should one talk with students and advisees about social class and being first-gen, and why is this important?

Visiting Scholar and Lecturer in Sociology Dwight Lang attends this meeting and finds the discussions to be quite fascinating—in particular, the university's apparent hesitance in acknowledging the presence of all students from lower- and working-class families. This overlaps with his long-term interests in American social class inequality—especially in higher education. Greg Merritt, Elise Bodei, and Dwight Lang become advisers to an informal first-gen group. Greg, Elise, Dwight, and Chyrisha begin speaking with students they know about forming a first-gen group.

# Winter

Five interested first-gen undergrads ("The Founding Five") and three advisers begin meeting every other week to discuss the formation and direction of a new first-gen group. A group motto is proposed and adopted—The Three Rs: *Recognize*, *Raise Awareness* of, and *Resolve* first generation student concerns. As students think about this motto, they also talk and dream about a future campus center devoted to the unique experiences and needs of Michigan's first-gen students.

# Spring

The "Founding Five" (Chyrisha Brown, Angel Martin, Dan Echlin, Johnny Pierce, and Brad Vermurlen) and advisers (Elise, Greg, and Dwight) meet at the Michigan Union pool hall (3rd floor) to celebrate—with three pizzas and large sodas—the end of the 2007–2008 academic year and the beginning of the small but energetic first-generation student group. Dwight Lang displays his long dormant, award-winning pool playing skills.

◆

# How It All Started

Greg Merritt

Greg Merritt, PhD
Speaker, Trainer,
Community Builder

"My dad just doesn't understand, and it's been a real challenge to talk with him." Chyrisha Brown (Rucker)—a first-gen undergraduate in 2007—told me about her family's views on her attending college at our first one-on-one meeting. I think, *Boy, do I understand this experience*, as it was also true of my family back in 1983. My instant reaction was what I often suggested to students: "Find others whom you can empathize and connect with—those whose experiences can help all of you to find positive solutions to your collective experiences."

I had been at the University of Michigan as Associate Director of University Housing for almost a decade when these conversations occurred and I certainly recognized my own identity of being first in my family to attend college. So I called Susan Wilson, then the Director of Student Groups. I was embarrassed to learn from her that despite having well over one thousand student groups at the university, not one of them specifically targeted first-generation college students. I thanked Susan and went back to Chyrisha, saying: "I'm sorry to inform you that there is no such group. However, I think you should start one." And this was the spark that began the first-generation students organization during the winter semester of 2007.

While Chyrisha and I were having these conversations, I was also helping a fellow staff member and graduate student, Elise Frankish (Bodei), find a valuable internship for her master's program in student affairs at Eastern Michigan University. We began talking about ways to partner with students and help this new group find its legs. We began to meet on a regular basis and saw that students who got involved in those first couple meetings were finding real kinship and connection. They were sharing important stories that resonated across gender, race, and other personal identities.

Elise and I had multiple conversations in those first months of 2007, when finding a time to meet was a real challenge due to the unique conditions of this population. The fact that many of the students had jobs on top of all of the other requirements of attending an elite institution like the University of Michigan meant that our meeting time would mosty likely be limited to 10–11 p.m. on Monday nights. I recall Elise saying at one point: "I don't know if they're going to make it." I responded with something to the effect of, "Listen, this is about a long-term strategy. Imagine what things will be like in ten to twenty years. This is a critically important identity for a place like Michigan if it intends to be the representative flagship public institution in the state. This must work to connect low-income students who are the first in their families to attend college so they can thrive in a place like this. This group can and will help those students, so try to be patient."

In early fall semester of 2007 we learned there was a staff groundswell of support that we simply didn't know about and hadn't tapped into yet. We decided we should have a meeting in a small conference room on the 6th floor at the newly constructed Palmer Commons building. The room was big enough for sixteen people and we didn't have a food or coffee budget. We wondered if we could borrow coffee from another group meeting next door! Nearly twenty-five people attended that first day! It was here that I met Dwight Lang for the first time and, with Elise, we became coadvisers to this brand new undergraduate group.

None of us had any idea the very first year-end celebration event (with five students and three advisors) in the pool hall at the Michigan Union would eventually evolve into the fully fledged, university-supported initiative it is today. The university now publicly welcomes and supports first-gens with a first-generation center and a full-time coordinator as well as a university-sponsored webpage. As I reflect on the time I've spent with so many of these talented students over the years, one thing stands out: I have always said to our first-gens, "Leverage your strengths. It's not a cliché to say that as first-gens, you are trailblazers, entrepreneurs, pioneers, and leaders who will forever change the culture of this fine institution."

I am proud to have experienced this journey with Chyrisha, Elise, and Dwight. I look forward to seeing on-going commitments from the University of Michigan to help first-gens thrive both as students and as alumni. I only hope the University of

Michigan will become known as the number one school in the world for first-gens! First-Generationally Yours.

◆

## Finding a Way

### Chyrisha Rucker (Brown)

When I stand in front of a mirror, my reflection tells conflicting stories: excellence and dissonance, achievements and failures, acceptance and disconnect, but mostly stories of determination and independence. Some people are able to choose their paths, and some paths are already chosen for them. The route we take aligns us with the greatest chance for reaching our potential and helps shape our worldviews and lives. Before college, my self-image was present but unclear, even hidden: it was obscured. This out-of-focus internal vision defined me before I knew what it really meant. I eventually came to know that blurred image as first-gen: the first in my family to attend college.

Chyrisha Brown
BA '09 Psychology and
Women's Studies
MBA '13 Conerstone
University
Program Manager, Detroit
Medical Center

During my first week on campus in the fall of 2006, I was a move-in maker: I helped students get settled in their dorm rooms.

I was also responsible for a lot of my educational costs and I used this platform to jump feet first into the "first-gens@Michigan" identity without realizing it. I found myself burdened with many questions and few answers. I didn't know who to talk to or what I should talk with them about. It was hard to find resources and I felt isolated and alone. So, in the vastness of my bewilderment and independence I applied to become a Resident Advisor (RA) because true independence came in the form of contributing to my college expenses. I connected with others by developing my resource base and gained a mentorship platform for myself and others.

A component of this new role was completing the RA training course. We learned about roles, tools, and strategies for handling conflict; explored cultural identities; and identified resources and opportunities for mentorship with the overall goal of providing a harmonious environment for students to grow, learn, and live on campus. On a particularly difficult day in the winter semester of 2007, I had a one-on-one mentoring session with Greg Merritt, a residential staff class facilitator. He listened to my gripes and offered some helpful tips. He also tapped into my regal side by asking me to do something about what I was feeling. Equal levels of determination and insecurity coursed through my body, and I thought: "Why don't I do something about it? Why don't I start a first-gen group?" And there, in West Quad's cafeteria, with the Cube spinning dismally outside the Michigan Union, our first-gens at Michigan brainstorming began.

The first step was making sure nothing like this already existed on campus, and we soon discovered that Michigan did not have any kind of first-generation student organization. Greg and I were in the process of developing a support group, a family consisting of people who shared the same first-gen identity. We quickly learned this was a controversial topic that went unaddressed by campus administrative offices. Talking about the first-gen experience seemed to be viewed by the university as isolating or maybe even discriminatory. I wondered why. But change was on the horizon! Greg connected me with other students and even brought the conversation to the attention of a staff member and graduate student, Elise Bodei.

Five students held meetings to develop the first-gen group concept. My most vivid winter 2008 memories were meetings with our advisers: Greg Merritt, Elise Bodei, and Dwight Lang. During late evening gatherings in reserved classrooms in Mason Hall we wrote out our goals and hopes. We, the "founding five," created the "three Rs." I can still see the red dry-erase marker lines on the classroom whiteboard. We wanted our group to display first-gens in a positive light. So that first-gen struggles could be *Recognized,* we sought to *Raise Awareness* and *Resolve* obstacles through mentorship, community, information, access, and security. Our group felt safe: it was our place of peace as the academic world swirled around us. We really didn't need others explaining to us what we already knew deep inside.

During that winter semester of 2008, we generated something concrete to take back our imagined powerlessness: the group reshaped our narratives—our way. We were not victims of our reflections or avoidance by the university. We were brazen images, greater than we ever imagined. In April 2008, we proudly held a billiards night in the Michigan Union to celebrate the end of another year on campus, where those who decided to join could celebrate group accomplishments and efforts.

The next step was to generate interest. We had a table at Festifall 2008 and wore shirts that asked, "Are you first?" People wanted to know more, and word spread across campus like wildfire. We completed the necessary paperwork to be formally recognized as a student organization and that was the tipping point of "the idea." We gained momentum by holding meetings every two weeks to talk about our greatest needs: developing stable programming, inviting guest speakers, and fostering relationships within the wider campus community. We held a backpacking party for winter 2009 class registration and participated in volunteer tutoring at a local community program for underprivileged youth. We were sowing seeds for the next generation of "first-gens" while receiving nourishment for our own growth. We established a board, further developed the website, wrote our own first-gen stories, and spent a few meetings sharing those stories. We felt strong and visible.

By winter 2009, as a graduating senior, I was proud of and overwhelmed by the work we had accomplished as well as the journey that lay ahead. The small graduation ceremony at Dwight Lang's home, the relationships we built, and the amount of knowledge we gained all supported our initial goals. I was energized by the notion that something could be done about the way I felt, about the problem that could not be easily identified. I was strengthened by a community of people looking to pave the way for others. The "founding five" (including Angel Martin, Brad Vermurlen, and me) had laid the foundation to make the college experience more manageable for students who had no one to guide them. To me, that was and is the first-gen way.

◆

# Clearing Hurdles

### Elise Bodei

The beginning of the First-Generation College Students@Michigan started with a September 2007 email sent to as many campus professionals as Greg Merritt and I could think of. The email advertised a meeting we were planning to discuss current issues facing first-gens at the University of Michigan here in Ann Arbor. We would talk about ways faculty and staff could start offering more support to our first-gens. I reserved a small conference room in Palmer Commons, thinking we would be lucky to have a handful of folks. The response was overwhelming! Not only was the room overflowing with 25–30 people, we also received emails from people who couldn't attend but wanted to become involved. Once we saw the amount of support for and interest in this idea, we knew there was something unique happening.

As we moved to assist students in starting the organization during the 2007–2008 academic year, we initially found there was less interest among students. It was difficult to get the fledgling group's members involved in attending events and meetings, which were initially held from 10 to 11 p.m. every other week in different Mason Hall classrooms. Students were also not sure which direction to take with their efforts. Should they focus on raising funds for first-gen scholarships? Financial resources to attend Michigan were certainly an important theme, but that turned out to be fraught with administrative hurdles. Did they have enough members to be able to produce an information brochure for new first-gens? Yes, probably. But it was difficult to squeeze in time to work on that, do work-study, and keep up with school without feeling burned out. Eventually, students settled on a three-pronged mission, later known as the "Three Rs:" *Recognize* the presence of first-gens on campus, *Raise awareness* of first-gen issues, and *Resolve* first-gen needs. This seemed to fit with what they felt was important and also was broad enough to cover what they had time to do and wanted to explore.

Over time, students realized the core of the first-gen experience was each individual's story. Everyone's journey to and life on campus was slightly different, but in hearing others' stories, they better understood their own journeys and began to feel empowered and supported. Similarly, sharing stories deepened their understanding of where they had come from and were going. Sharing stories was empowering and liberating for many. Students came to hear and share stories, to learn, and to be reminded they weren't alone at Michigan, even if their experiences were different from those of their more affluent peers.

We continued to encounter hurdles. Getting word out about the group and attracting students from diverse identities and backgrounds was one challenge. Especially frustrating for me was the lack of available information on exactly how many first-gens were on campus. The Registrar refused to release the information due to a fear that it was "stigmatizing," even reported as an aggregate number. Despite this institutional roadblock, students in our group were victorious and inspiring in so many other ways. To us, "first-gen" was something to be super proud of.

As time went on, the group was able to get more support from the Department of Sociology, the Office of the Provost, and, eventually, Student Life. This led to more organized social and academic events highlighting first-gen stories, togetherness, and community which were very important to first-gen students and their families.

In August 2018, I logged into the College of Literature, Science, and Arts SSA Management Reporting System, an in-house staff portal for data of all kinds. There is a new data reporting feature at the top of the portal that currently reports enrollment data according to various groups: the number of students enrolled, the number of first-year students enrolled, the number of transfer students, and, in its own group, *the number of enrolled first-gens and first-gen transfer students.* I was stunned!

We have moved from being unable to obtain a report from the Registrar's Office of how many first-gen students there were on campus in 2008 to currently reporting first-gen figures—unsolicited—to all staff through a central system. And that's not to mention the many other amazing things that have taken off after that very first meeting with faculty and staff, as well as the 10 p.m. meetings in the winter of 2008. We now have a first-gen center in the Office of Academic and Multicultural Initiatives (First-Generation Student Gateway) and a full-time first-gen coordinator as well as welcome and graduation events for hundreds of first-gen students and their families.

—*Elise Bodei '00, Chief Administrator,*
*Department of Communication Studies,*
*University of Michigan, Ann Arbor*

# 4

# 2008–2009

## Fall

First-gen tables are set up at Festifall 2008 to announce group happenings and membership initiatives, and similar plans are made for Winterfest 2009. These campus events allow all interested student groups to advertise their activities. In the years to follow, students continue participating in Festifalls and Winterfests. Both "fests" help recruit new members and raise awareness of first-gen issues.

Interested first-gens and advisers continue meeting on a regular basis to chart directions and campus activities. *Greg Merritt* and *Elise Bodei* are able to attend most meetings. *Dwight Lang* is able to attend every meeting and joins students for all evening meetings through the winter semester of 2019. Advisers are always available to talk one-on-one with students during the week. They witness the various challenges and accomplishments of Michigan's first-generation students and encourage them to be proud of their social class heritage. Together, they see this background as a unique and powerful strength. Students choose a name for the group: *First-Generation College Students@Michigan* (FGCS@M). FGCS@M spearheads an early and informal grassroots initiative to shine a light on this visible yet largely unacknowledged group of students on campus.

FGCS@M students visit the registrar's office to determine how many first-gen undergrads are enrolled at Michigan. They are told that the registrar's office does not release this type of information because being first-gen is a negative stigma. Students wonder how or if they should identify themselves to peers, staff, and faculty and if they do, what are the related risks and consequences. Students and advisers wonder if this is also the wider administration's view. Dwight Lang wonders how African-American and Hispanic students in 1968 or 1969 would have reacted to the registrar's office telling them that their enrollment numbers would not be released because being Black or Hispanic involved a negative stigma.

The fact that being a first-generation college student is immediately associated with negative stigmas (e.g., being poor and working-class) is particularly troublesome and painful for FGCS@M students, especially given their positive experiences growing up in homes with supportive family members. Does the university pity them or view them as inferior to their peers because of their low-income background? Does the university really want them to be here? These harmful perceptions actually become powerful how first-gens seem to be viewed at Michigan—out of sight, out of mind, invisible, and sources of embarrassment. First-gen advisers are pleased to see this first-gen motivation and encourage students to be proud of their social class heritage.

## October/November

Students apply to be officially recognized as an undergraduate organization by the *Michigan Student Assembly*. Organizational status is granted and students are very happy. They determine, after various internet searches, that FGCS@M is likely the first undergraduate group at an American college or university to focus on students who are the first in their families to attend or graduate from a four-year college.

Professor and Department of Sociology Chair *Howard Kimeldorf* supports a departmental recognition of FGCS@M. This is very important considering that there are very few first-gen Michigan undergraduates in 2008–2009, and that the university might view being first-gen as a negative stigma. This departmental acknowledgment is the first formal institutional effort to help raise awareness of first-gen issues, and students are very pleased the sociology department publicly recognizes their presence on campus.

Students and advisers meet with the department chair and administrators, and the Department of Sociology sponsors FGCS@M ("a student organization recognized by the Michigan Student Assembly"). The *Agreement of Sponsorship*, in part, reads: "The sponsoring relationship encourages University academic departments ... to support the potential of student organizations to actively contribute to the cultural, social, and academic life on campus."

The sociology department offers the following resources to FGCS@M: office space (3147 LSA); a staff adviser, *Elise Bodei (Frankish)*, who would act as liaison to the Department of Sociology and the wider campus community and provide leadership counseling; use of the photocopier to print flyers; supplies for meetings and events (paper plates, cups, napkins); and a discretionary budget of $200 per academic year. FGCS@M also receives two anonymous contributions in support of the group's activities. On December 3, 2008, the Department of Sociology and members of the *First-Generation College Students@Michigan* meet to sign the *Agreement of Sponsorship* (see Appendix). The following individuals sign the Agreement: Department of Sociology Chair *Howard Kimeldorf,* Department Manager *Jennifer Eshelman,* Undergraduate Program Coordinator and FGCS@M Adviser *Elise Frankish,* Lecturer and FGCS@M Faculty Adviser *Dwight Lang* and nine undergraduate students: *Aimee Von Bakel, Chyrisha Brown, Alexa DiFiore, Aimrie Ream, Carley Flanery, Lauren Sterrett, Sara Pikora, Candyce Hill, Kristin Lo.*

♦

# My Decision to Support First-Generation College Students@Michigan

Howard Kimeldorf

Howard Kimeldorf, PhD
Professor Emeritus
Department of Sociology
University of Michigan,
Ann Arbor

I was Chair of the Department of Sociology in 2008 when Elise Frankish, our undergraduate adviser, and Dwight Lang, one of our lecturers, asked the Department to formally sponsor First-Generation College Students@Michigan—a routine requirement to secure University recognition—and, if possible, also provide a space for their monthly meetings.

I agreed to support the first-gen group based on two principles, one more abstract and the other practical. The first stemmed from my long-held belief that the University of Michigan, being a public institution, should be committed to serving the state's residents, whose tax dollars help support its educational and research missions. One way of delivering on that commitment is by making the University accessible to Michigan's top students and ensuring that the student body's composition mirror the state's population as much as possible. Among the groups most often underrepresented at Michigan and other highly selective institutions are students who are first in their families to attend college. First-gens deserved my support for raising the issue of underrepresentation for this largely overlooked group of students.

I also supported our first-gens as a more practical matter, believing that the University had an obligation to create something approximating a level playing field for all students. A large body of research demonstrates that first-generation college students, who typically lack the family-based informational, cultural, and monetary resources available to their more affluent peers, are at a distinct disadvantage trying to navigate the unfamiliar and at times alien environment of college, both inside and outside the classroom. First-gens earned my support for addressing this problem by creating a supportive setting where students could share their informal knowledge while developing a stronger sense of their own belonging on campus.

I am beyond pleased to see that First-Generation College Students@Michigan has met with such success, outgrowing its initial sponsorship and housing within the Department of Sociology. It is now a University-sponsored organization with its own dedicated space, staff, and institutionally recognized mission of making Michigan more open and inviting to all first-generation college students.

◆

# Winter

Dwight Lang invites Department of Anthropology Chair Thomas Fricke, a fellow first-gen college graduate, to attend a meeting and talk about his own journey to an academic career and a middle-class life. He reflects on growing up in North Dakota, starting college at Bismarck Community College, and eventually completing his PhD at the University of Wisconsin–Madison. Besides Dwight Lang, Professor Fricke is the only other first-gen faculty member students have the opportunity to talk with and discuss social science research. Tom describes the intricacies and challenges of deciding to pursue an academic career. His presentation has an impact on students and shows that first-gens can have accomplished careers.

FGCS@M is featured in an essay in College of Literature, Science, and the Arts's *LSA Magazine* written by Dwight Lang: "First-Generation Students: A New Campus Organization Helps Those Who Are the First in Their Family to Attend College" (Spring 2009, p. 49). FGCS@M adviser Greg Merritt is quoted in the essay: "This diverse group—white, African American, Hispanic, male and female, urban and rural—explores a range of issues from what to expect living in residence halls, to interacting in classrooms, to how to talk with a professor, to how to buy books, and more." Fellow adviser Elise Frankish comments that the group exists to help first-gens resolve concerns such as communicating with family about school-related issues and adjusting to their new lives on campus. "The overarching goal is always to enhance student success." This *LSA Magazine* story is the first media source to acknowledge the presence of first-generation students at Michigan and helps raise awareness of first-gen issues, especially feelings of difference and isolation.

First-gen end of year celebration, 1118 Wells Street, 2009

Dwight and Sylvia Lang

# April

FGSC@M students meet at Dwight and Sylvia Lang's Ann Arbor home for the first time to celebrate the end of the academic year. There is one 2009 graduate in FGSC@M—Chyrisha Brown. Students learn that both Dwight and Sylvia are first in their families to attend and graduate from college: Dwight graduated with a BA in 1972 and completed his PhD in 1983, and Sylvia graduated with a BA in 1974 and completed her PhD in 1983.

# Summer

Dwight Lang runs into Emeritus Professor of Sociology Mayer Zald at an Ann Arbor bank at the corner of Washtenaw Avenue and Huron River Drive. Professor Zald comments that he's very pleased with the spring issue of *LSA Magazine* and Dwight Lang's essay on first-gens at Michigan. He tells Lang that he is also a first-gen and Dwight asks if Mayer would like to attend an FGCS@M meeting in the fall to talk about his own first-gen journey. Professor Zald says he'd be delighted to do so.

# 5

## 2009–2010

## Fall

FGCS@M begins meeting twice per month throughout the academic year to chart the group's direction and develop strategies to expand membership. Members and advisers regularly discuss what it means to be first-gen at the University of Michigan—the beginning of their middle-class journeys. Topics include but are not limited to first-gen identity and how it intersects with race, ethnicity, gender, and sexual orientation; rural and urban backgrounds; nuclear and extended family relationships during early stages of upward mobility; plans for career and graduate and professional schools; and finding first-gen role models at the university. These topics—as related to first-gen experiences—have not been covered by various Student Life offices, activities, or presentations on campus. Students wonder why and discuss how to address these oversights.

A second FGCS@M motto is proposed by first-gen Danielle Miller and is adopted: *We may be the first, but we won't be the last.*

◆

## Why We May Be the First, but We Won't Be the Last

### Danielle Miller

Danielle Miller
BA '11 Microbiology
Georgia Department of Public Health
Emergency Preparedness and Response

When I joined First-Gens@Michigan in the fall of 2007, I was a pretty introverted kid. I shrank away from outreach events, like Festifall on the Diag, where we had to compete with all the other student organizations to intrigue students enough to visit our table and, ultimately, join our club. I loved our group meetings, however, and thrived in a small group setting, just brainstorming with fellow students and advisers about what we wanted to be and wanted to accomplish. That's why somewhere around the fall of 2009, after our numbers had grown some and we felt compelled to split the group into subcommittees to be a better and more effective club, I volunteered to maintain our website.

Since FGCS@M's inception, we envisioned a group that not only raised awareness of the first-gen identity but also provided new tools and resources for current and future first-gens to succeed. We remembered our own struggles and wanted to do what we could to lessen the burden for future generations. I began researching resources to include on our site as well as other first-generation student clubs at other universities with whom we could connect and perhaps form a supportive network. A couple groups with an online presence mentioned first-gens, but it wasn't their focus. This felt like a grain of sand in the vast ocean that is the internet, and it seemed outrageous because I knew there must be more of us out there. First-generation college students may have been a minority at most colleges and universities, but we still made up a considerable percentage of the student population nationwide.

But maybe the first-gen presence both online and in student organizations was so small because it is a fairly "invisible" identity marker. During another group brainstorming session, we found a new project in curating stories for the website: a collection of personal essays by our members that spoke to the power and experience of being first-gen. In addition to being a place for academic and financial resources, we wanted our website to represent the first-gen identity, to give a face to this invisible demographic by highlighting the diversity and personal experiences of those who identified as first-gen. I thought about the need not just for accessible information but for a bigger voice for first-gens everywhere.

This made a lot of sense. Our group meetings often ended with us swapping anecdotes that spoke directly to the experiences of being the first in our families to attend college. And as I worked more on the website, scouring the internet for others like us, and collected more essays for our stories project, I began to wonder: "What does it mean to be among the first of this collective identity to raise our voices across the entire collegiate community in America, to be pioneers laying a foundation upon which those among us and those who came after of us could use to succeed?" I realized we were not just forging familial legacies—we were hopefully, even if not consciously, creating a community that would inspire and prepare future first-gens for generations to come: "We may be the first, but we won't be the last."

◆

# Winter

Dwight Lang invites Michigan Emeritus Professor of Sociology and fellow first-gen Mayer Zald to attend a meeting to describe his journey to a middle-class career as an academic. He talks about growing up in a Detroit neighborhood where very few children thought about attending college. He started college at Wayne State University in Detroit and transferred to Michigan to complete his bachelor's degree ('53). After finishing his master's in sociology at the University of Hawaii ('55), he returned to the University of Michigan to complete his PhD ('61). Students are pleased to hear about Professor Zald's first-gen history and surprised by the fact that many first-gens, like Professor Zald, attended the University of Michigan in the 1950's. His inspirational talk showed that first-gens can also realize dreams and goals.

Vice Provost for Academic Affairs—Lester Monts provides the

first two-year grant (2010–2012) to support FGCS@M campus activities. The application is submitted by Dwight Lang with Howard Kimeldorf's support. This funding represents another important institutional support for recognizing first-gen presence and conditions. FGCS@M students are somewhat surprised with this financial support and are inspired to carry-on during the next academic year.

Students choose the first executive board—consisting of a president, vice president, secretary, and treasurer—for the 2010–2011 academic year. Angelica "Angel" Martin ('12) is elected the first president of FGCS@M. Angel was also one of the "founding five" that met during the winter semester of 2008.

First-gen gathering, April 2010

# April

FGSC@M students meet again at *Dwight and Sylvia Lang's* home to celebrate the end of the academic year. There are no FGSC@M graduates for 2009–10.

◆

## Group Culture and Structure

### Angelica "Angel" Martin

During the first term of my freshman year (fall 2007), I came to the jarring realization that I was grossly unprepared for college. In those early months, I acknowledged that my educational training prior to college was lacking, so much so that my 4.0 high school GPA was roughly equivalent to a 2.5 GPA at the University of Michigan. I came to appreciate how social inequalities—rooted in social constructs, economic disparities, and cultural identities—largely accounted for this unpreparedness. I coped with new identities such as "culturally black" and "first-generation college student" (first-gen). I learned how to exist in what seemed like two completely different worlds: my home community and my new academic community.

Angelica Martin
BA '12 Biochemistry
PhD '17 Pharmacology and Cancer Biology
Duke University
Manager, Grants and Special Projects
Emerson Collective Health Team

Being first-gen puts you at a social disadvantage because it is a social inequality posing unique challenges to your success. As a second- or third-generation college student—especially multigenerational Michigan Wolverines—family members can easily show you the ropes. They have a built-in support system that instills the confidence needed to achieve and thrive. Loved ones are always there to remind these students that college is an experience one is entitled to, an automatic stepping stone to success. Contrast that with my experience. My family, as encouraging and supportive as any, could only express how proud they were that I had endured enough K–12 schooling to take on college. My support system lacked the intellectual and social capital that proves vital for ensuring strong academic performance and personal satisfaction. Without this insight, first-gens experience higher attrition rates because they endured insurmountable barriers to success.

During my first semester, I was fortunate to find kindred spirits who were also looking to confront these unique first-gen challenges. Together, as the "founding five," we established the student-led organization First-Generation College Students@Michigan, one of the first of its kind in the nation. Our goals were to recognize, raise awareness, and resolve the needs of first-gen students at Michigan.

As one of the founders, I helped build the group's infrastructure. As the first president of FGCS@M (2010–2011), my greatest challenge was to help shape our group's culture and structure. It was particularly challenging to reconcile a group vision. The majority of members wanted space to discuss first-gen issues and connect with peers. I and a few others wanted a more formal structure to establish a long-term institutional presence as a means to garner university support. It was essential, I felt, to broaden our impact on the campus community beyond our interpersonal connections. Most importantly, I was determined to prevent future first-gens from feeling invalidated and invisible due to their first-gen identity.

To sway the majority to adopt this vision, I encouraged them to have a trial period whereby group members assumed different administrative roles. These roles created an organizational structure enabling us to implement programming (e.g., publications, advising, and information on access to campus resources; recruiting members and garnering support from the university) and maintain a space for dialogue and community building. As the first elected president of the group, I worked diligently to bring our vision to fruition. I met with university administrators to generate funds for recruitment and outreach events and I led campus-wide staff workshops to raise awareness of first-gen needs.

The group's infrastructure (e.g., the executive board and advisers) that I helped establish is still an organizational pillar and guiding framework for the group today. This structure has enabled great success for FGCS@M over the years, triumphs that included working with the university administration to list "first-gen" as an identity category on student surveys given to incoming freshmen. Students who check this box are now routed to our group and are made aware of available community and resources before they matriculate.

First-gen success has proven critical to my overall growth. I have continued my life pursuits with an enthusiasm and diligence fostered, in large part, by my experiences as a founder, member, and former president of FGCS@M. I continue serving as a leader in my communities, including my diverse biomedical graduate and business communities as well as my local community. FGCS@MI served as a unique training opportunity in effective leadership and teamwork, training that has proven indispensable for my professional development.

# 6

## 2010–2011

## Fall

After Festifall, FGCS@M continues meeting twice a month to discuss group direction, membership expansion, and first-gen issues on and off campus. Membership grows. Students discuss the possibility of establishing a first-generation student center, similar to the Multi Ethnic Student Affairs Office (MESA), the Office of Academic and Multicultural Initiatives (OAMI), or the Comprehensive Studies Program (CSP). Since CSP serves some first-gens, FGCS@M students and Dwight Lang approach CSP staff to determine if there might be cooperation between CSP and FGCS@M to better serve all first-gens. CSP states that it is not interested in collaborating with FGCS@M.

# Winter

Students establish a Facebook page and a mailing list to improve communications and planning initiatives for all UM first-gen students. These virtual communication tools are particularly important because not all students can attend evening meetings due to work-study responsibilities. But everyone can keep up and potentially help with what the group is doing on campus.

Professor Alford Young becomes chair of the sociology department in the fall of 2010 and continues essential departmental support for FGCS@M. Dwight Lang asks Al Young to attend the last meeting of the 2010–2011 academic year in Mason Hall, where he reaffirms departmental support for this new undergraduate group. Students greatly appreciate Professor Young's inspirational comments regarding how first-gens are changing the University of Michigan's landscape. A group photo is taken.

Students choose a new executive board for the 2011–2012 academic year. Carley Flanery ('12; MSW and MPH '14) is elected president.

# April

Three FGCS@M graduates and their parents, as well as other first-gen students, meet in the Pond Room at the Michigan Union to celebrate graduation and the end of the academic year. Angel Martin and Carley Flanery reflect on group accomplishments and plans for the coming academic year. The fact that a critical number of first-gens have become involved in FGCS@M is highlighted and recognized as a major source of pride.

First-gen Graduation, April 2011

◆

# Being First-Gen

Carley Flanery

I became a member of First-Generation College Students@Michigan in September 2008, which is also when I "found out" I was first-gen. Where I grew up (Crandon, Wisconsin), nearly everyone would have been a first-gen if they had attended college. So it wasn't a salient identity for me until I arrived in Ann Arbor. As a member I gained friendships, strengthened existing ones because of our shared first-gen identities, and gained invaluable leadership experiences.

As president during the 2011–2012 academic year, the mentorship I received from older student members and the former president, as well as our faculty and staff advisers, propelled me into spaces I couldn't have imagined without their guidance and support. One event I'll always remember is our third-annual campus graduation celebration in the Michigan Union (April 2013). UM Vice President for Global Communications and Strategic Initiatives Lisa Rudgers gave the keynote address, which was huge for us. Twenty-five people (including parents and siblings) attended, if I remember correctly, including first-gen graduates and their families. This was our largest graduation celebration since the formation of First-Generation College Students@Michigan in 2008.

Carley Flanery
BA '12 Sociology
MSW and MPH '14
Director, Office of
Sexual Assault and
Relationship Abuse
Education
Stanford University

# 7

## 2OII–2OI2

## Fall

First-gen tables are set up at Festifall 2011 (and later at Winterfest 2012) announcing group activities and membership activities. Large banners publicizing FGCS@M are hung around the Diag in late August and remain through the first month of classes. FGCS@M membership continues to grow after the annual mass meeting in September.

First-gen table at Festifall (Anna Garcia, left, and Theresa Johnson)

First-gen meeting, Fall 2011

First-gen undergraduates continue reaching out to staff regarding first-gen experiences. First-gen graduate students are asked to attend bimonthly meetings to discuss graduate school application plans and graduate student life. UM first-gen faculty members are invited to discuss academic career options and how to plan for graduate and/or professional school life and professional careers. Professor David Tucker from the School of Social Work attends a meeting in Mason Hall to talk about his own first-gen journey and make suggestions regarding any graduate school plans.

Jessi Streib, a graduate student in sociology, attends a meeting in the Michigan League to describe her dissertation research examining long-term cross-class marriages. This is the first time students have heard about detailed academic research during monthly meetings. Jessi does a great job of explaining the research process and some of her early findings.

Halloween 2011

Students meet to carve pumpkins for Halloween. This fall activity continues in future years.

At monthly meetings, conversations often revolve around adjustments to a middle- and upper-middle-class campus atmosphere, as well as ongoing family interactions and the nature of first-gen, upward social class mobility. Some students still struggle to explain college life, expectations, and experiences to parents, siblings, and extended family members who have not attended college. Some parents appear worried about losing sons or daughters to another way of life (a middle-class world) they have little knowledge of or do not trust. Students conclude they should reach out more to family members to explain courses they're taking and their developing upward mobility as well as the new social class where they're planning to live. This is hard work, but students feel it is necessary in order to maintain family relationships and continuity.

# Winter

Vice Provost for Academic Affairs Lester Monts provides a second two-year grant (2012–2014) to support FGCS@M campus activities. Dwight Lang submits the application with Al Young's support. This funding represents important and ongoing institutional support for FGCS@M.

Dwight Lang approaches The Ann Arbor News about possibly writing a story about FGCS@M. The News editor suggests an article coauthored by first-gens. The story, written by students Danielle Boshers, Anna Garcia, Melody Ng, and Chris Reynolds, as well as adviser Dwight Lang, is published in the April 19th edition: "First-Generation College Students at Michigan Share Their Stories." Dwight Lang writes, "The four students writing the essays below are current members of First-Gens @ Michigan and share vital elements of their journeys to higher education. They review very real challenges, but also identify special, yet familiar first-gen strengths that help them explore new social places. Their experiences reflect a wide range of difficulties many colleges and universities frequently face when publicly acknowledging social class difference. This type of social diversity impacts students in multiple ways. These first-gen students make visible what is too often invisible." This *Ann Arbor News* article publicly addresses first-gen issues in Ann Arbor and at the University of Michigan.

Students choose a new executive board for the 2012–2013 academic year. Carson Philips ('14) is elected president.

First-gen Graduation, Michigan Union, April 2012

# April

Five FGCS@M graduates and their parents, as well as other first-gen students, meet in the Michigan Union to celebrate graduation and the end of the academic year. *Malinda Matney*, Director of Assessment, Center for Research on Learning and Teaching, College of Education, gives the keynote address. Malinda talks about her own first-gen journey and advises students to be proud of their own journeys and accomplishments here at the University of Michigan.

◆

## *Expanding and Raising Awareness*

### Carson Philips

I am privileged to have served as the president of First-Generation College Students@Michigan for two years (2012–2014). I am also grateful to have worked with such a supportive and diligent executive board to achieve several key milestones. Throughout my tenure, the organization focused largely on increasing membership and building greater capacity for the organization's work. To do so, we relied heavily on raising awareness of social class issues among more privileged students and building partnerships with other student organizations.

We encountered difficulties that stemmed from trying to find a clear and specific purpose. For some students, the organization operated as an advocacy group that sought to garner greater support from campus administrators. For example, I regularly attended fireside chats with then-President Mary Sue Coleman and spoke about first-gens to turn greater administrative attention toward first-gen issues and concerns. For other students, participation in our group was a way to find community with peers who came from similar social class backgrounds. Other students joined the organization with plans to give back through community service to local high schools. Ultimately, it was this tripartite mission that led our organization to experience significant membership growth between 2012 and 2014.

Carson Philips
BA '14 Sociology and African American Studies
MA '16 Educational Policy and Leadership Studies
University of Iowa
Institutional Researcher, Office of Budget and Planning
University of Michigan, Ann Arbor

There is also power in storytelling, so several meetings each semester were devoted to sharing stories about our journeys through higher education and our experiences as undergraduates. Through these stories, first-gens were able to see they were not alone in their challenges and that there were ways to support one another in our endeavors and ultimately achieve our goals.

The University of Michigan has begun to address the unique needs of first-generation college students, but there is much more work to be done. The university needs to acknowledge that it is not just educating students and providing them with credentials but rather changing life outcomes of students and their kin for many generations to come. The post-collegiate experiences of many students are a testament to how the university is engaged in promoting students' upward mobility. The university should be honored to be playing such an important role in first-generation college students' lives. After all, we may be the first, but we won't be the last.

# 8

## 2012–2013

----

## Fall

First-gen undergraduates continue reaching out to UM staff regarding the first-gen campus experience. Students visit the Office of First-Year Programs (OFYP) to discuss how first-gen experiences might be recognized and incorporated into the summer orientation programs for all first-year students. Students feel this would help first-gens feel more included in campus culture during their first semester and assist more affluent students to better understand social class diversity. OFYP agrees to identify and discuss first-gen status and experiences during annual orientation programs held in late summer. FGCS@M students are particularly happy with OFYP's decision in that many first-gen freshmen often experience serious adjustment problems during their early weeks and months on campus, difficulties that too often lead to first-gens dropping out.

First-gens, Mason Hall, Fall 2012

Dwight Lang approaches the Instructional Technology office about featuring FGCS@M on the first page of the UM website. FGSC@M is highlighted for seven days.

The *Michigan Daily* student newspaper publishes an October 4 article by Alicia Adamczyk titled: "Group Unites First-Generation College Students on Campus." FGCS@M member Theresa Johnson talks about being unable to call her parents for advice. She says it can be hard for first-gens to feel comfortable at the university, "since they aren't accustomed to the system." Carson Philips comments: "We just try to present our group as a resource for other students and support and help them. I think one of the biggest struggles for most first-gens is the lack of a support network." Reflecting on the impact the group has on students, FGCS@M adviser Elise Bodei remarks that she has "heard many students say having first-gens as a place to go, even if only to listen, made the difference in their Michigan experience. Sometimes it even helped them make the decision to stay enrolled when they considered transferring or leaving school."

Elise Bodei leaves the Department of Sociology for a new administrative position in the Department of Political Science. She continues in her role as FGCS@M adviser, but in a reduced capacity. She eventually moves on to the Departments of Physics and Communications Studies, but remains a very strong first-gen advocate. Her contributions to the early years of FGCS@M will always be fondly remembered.

Carving pumpkins

Students meet to carve pumpkins for Halloween.

FGCS@M partners with the off-campus Family Learning Institute tutoring low-income elementary and middle school students in Ann Arbor. This association continues in coming years.

Carson Phillips regularly attends fireside chats with UM President Mary Sue Coleman. These meetings allow undergraduates to ask President Coleman about a variety of campus issues. At a December 2012 meeting, Carson speaks with President Coleman about the university's attention to first-gen issues and requests official statistics about their rates of enrollment, retention, and graduation. President Coleman refers his questions to Vice President for Student Life E. Royster Harper, who connects him with Malinda Matney, who was a researcher in the Office of Student Life at the time. At this point, there is minimal institutional research being conducted on first-gen issues and statistics (e.g., retention and graduation rates) are not readily available. The executive board continues reaching out to the university community regarding FGCS@M goals and activities.

# Winter

The Admission's Office Director of Marketing and Communications Betsy Brown attends a meeting to hear more about FGCS@M's goals. FGCS@M will be featured in recruitment materials as the Admissions Office expands efforts to reach out to high school seniors—and future college first-gens—around the state of Michigan.

Carson Philips ('14) and the 2012–2013 executive board remain in office for the 2013–2014 academic year.

# April

Lisa Rudgers

Numerous FGCS@M graduates and their parents, as well as other first-gen students, meet in the Michigan Union to celebrate graduation and the end of the academic year. UM Vice President for Global Communications and Strategic Initiatives Lisa Rudgers (a first-gen) gives the graduation keynote address. Lisa remembers her own years as a first-gen undergraduate and acknowledges the unique strengths first-gens bring to campus.

# 9

## 2013–2014

---

## Fall

First-gen undergraduates continue reaching out to UM staff regarding the first-gen campus experiences. Bimonthly meetings, sometimes with graduate and professional students, provide useful information about life in graduate and professional school.

First-gens, Michigan League, Fall 2013

Dwight Lang again asks the Instructional Technology office to feature FGCS@M on the home page of the University of Michigan's website. FGCS@M is highlighted for seven days.

## Winter

Vice Provost for Diversity, Equity, and Inclusion Rob Sellers provides a third two-year grant (2014–2016) to support FGCS@M campus activities. Dwight Lang submits the application, with Al Young's support. The grant represents ongoing institutional support for FGCS@M.

Students choose a new executive board for the 2014–2015 academic year. Anna Garcia ('15 and currently finishing her second year of medical school in the College of Human Medicine at Michigan State University) is elected president.

# April

FGCS@M students invite University Provost Martha Pollack to give the keynote address at the first-gen graduation ceremony. She accepts and students are pleased to know that the highest levels of the university's administration are becoming more aware of the first-gen experience and population.

Dwight Lang meets with Martha Pollack to personally thank her for agreeing to speak at the first-gen graduation ceremony. They discuss first-gen challenges at selective universities like Michigan, including feelings of invisibility and marginality on a campus where the majority of students, faculty, and staff have middle- and upper-middle-class backgrounds. She is pleased to hear that

Martha Pollack

First-Generation College Students@Michigan is sponsored by the Department of Sociology and financially supported by Vice Provost Rob Sellers. She expresses confidence this support will continue in the future and suggests the university should publicly acknowledge the presence of first-gen students.

The largest ever first-gen graduation ceremony—with a free dinner for students and families—is held in the Anderson Room at the Michigan Union. For the first time, Comprehensive Studies Program first-gens attend. FGCS@MI students are understandably pleased beyond belief. Approximately forty students and their parents are present. Provost Martha Pollack, a first-gen and current president of Cornell University, gives a heartfelt keynote address congratulating first-gen graduates and remembering her own first-gen undergraduate and graduate school days. Martha

Pollack's acknowledgement of FGCS@M's long-term efforts represents a critical turning point for institutional recognition of Michigan's first-generation student experiences.

First-gen Graduation, advisers and e-board members, April 2014

## Summer

Carson Philips ('14) works as an intern for Assistant Vice Provost for Academic Affairs Dilip Das in the Office of the Vice Provost for Equity, Inclusion, and Academic Affairs. There, he conducts research on the conditions of first-generation college students. In fall 2014 Malinda Matney from the Office of Student Life publishes some statistics on first-generation undergraduates at the University of Michigan. Of the undergraduate population, 10.6% are considered first-generation students; 5.4% have parents who have never attended college, and 5.2% have parents who have completed some college. This appears to be the first time first-gen information is made publicly available online.

# 10

# 2014–2015

----

## September

Dwight Lang receives an email request from Vice-Provost for Diversity, Equity and Inclusion Rob Sellers to make an appointment to discuss first-gen conditions at the University of Michigan. They talk for two hours about a variety of first-generation experiences and challenges as well as various forms of social stratification in higher education. Vice-Provost Sellers is particularly interested in first-gen feelings of invisibility and marginality. He comments that the university will be making additional efforts to promote and ensure first-gen inclusion in campus culture.

"The Rock" at the corner of Hill Street and Washtenaw

Avenue is painted to announce the proud existence of First-Generation College Students@Michigan.

Danielle Boshers, Anna Garcia, and Chris Reynolds

# Winter

Dwight Lang contacts Jennifer Guerra about meeting to discuss a potential interview segment on WUOM, Michigan's local National Public Radio (NPR) station in Ann Arbor: State of Opportunity. Jennifer Guerra interviews FGCS@M members Anna Garcia, Chris Reynolds and Danielle Boshers and writes an article about first-generation college student experiences. The program airs on WUOM in early February 2015 and is immediately picked up by national NPR on February 16th and broadcast to the nation as "Fitting in on Campus: Challenges for First-Generation Students." Anna Garcia discusses starting college at Michigan: "It was hard for other students to understand that for us to go to college we were taking a big risk. ... I know of many students who have left after their freshmen year because they just felt they couldn't find their place on campus." Chris Reynolds never forgot his first few days as a freshman: "He wasn't prepared for how lonely and out of place he felt on campus. People would ask questions: 'What do my parents do?' or 'Where did they go to college?' His parents didn't go to college. His mom was a housekeeper and his dad was unemployed. Reynolds's responses were met with 'Oh' and 'OK.' " This important local and national media exposure highlights important first-gen issues at the University of Michigan and at similar colleges and universities around the country.

Assistant Vice-Provost for Academic Affairs Dilip Das and Dwight Lang initiate monthly meetings held at the Vice-Provost's Office for Diversity, Equity, and Inclusion with interested staff from various student affairs offices (e.g. the Career Center, the Office of First Year Programs, the Office of Financial Aid, Counseling and Psychological Services, and Multi-Ethnic Student Affairs). They share information regarding how each office interacts and

Dilip Das

communicates with and supports first-generation students. Networks begin to form around how best to serve first-gens, how to talk with first-gens about issues they must confront (e.g., a sense of isolation or feeling invisible), and developing productive measures to help first-gens feel comfortable and more welcome.

People attending these meetings suggest that first-generation status should not be viewed as a negative stigma. Staff members address faculty and staff unwarranted misconceptions and misgivings about lower-income students. Staff also talks about returning to their home offices and "spreading the word" about first-gen perspectives and experiences. This group comes to be known as the First-Generation Student Group (FGSG). FGCS@M students are invited to attend FGSG meetings on a regular basis, signifying important and joint administration/student efforts to recognize first generation challenges. FGSG represents additional institutional attention to the needs and conditions of Michigan's first-generation students. FGCS@M students note how far the university has come in recognizing the presence of first-gens.

With FGCS@M, the Vice-Provost for Diversity, Equity, and Inclusion Rob Sellers cosponsors the first winter semester first-gen dinner in the Michigan Union Rogel Ballroom. Vice-Provost Sellers addresses those in attendance, graciously welcoming students and acknowledging the importance of their presence at the University of Michigan. He clarifies that first-gens deserve to be at the University of Michigan and represent a vital component of the student body. Approximately eighty first-gen students attend—some with their children—and many share their sometimes difficult experiences and memories, especially feelings of invisibility. Crystal Flynn, an executive assistant in the Office of the Vice Provost for Diversity, Equity, and Inclusion, makes all needed arrangements for this dinner (including reserving the room and ordering food and a delicious cake). Crystal Flynn and Sylvia Lang greet all students as they enter Rogel Ballroom and continue this welcoming practice during future first-gen dinners and graduation ceremonies.

University of Michigan Vice President for Global Communications and Strategic Initiatives Lisa Rudgers initiates an upcoming, one-year (2015–2016), campus-wide campaign to raise awareness of and recognize first generation experiences/issues. FGCS@M is designated as the client of Michigan Creative–a University of Michigan office providing professional, creative, and communication services. *Dwight Lang* and first-gen students regularly meet with personnel from *Michigan Creative* to discuss strategies to help acknowledge and support first generation students.

A new executive board is chosen for the 2015–2016 academic year. Katherine "Katie" Thomas ('16) is elected president.

# April

Another large graduation ceremony and dinner for first-gen graduates and their families is held in the Michigan Union Rogel Ballroom. Approximately eighty students and their parents are present.

◆

## *Realizing First-Gen Pride*

### Katherine "Katie" Thomas

During the 2015–2016 academic year, I was president of the First-Generation College Students@Michigan group. This was a pivotal year for first-generation college students. First-gens were finally starting to feel they were being recognized and acknowledged by the university administration after having spent years blending in with the rest of the student body. Not only was there an increase in recognition but also increased participation in the group at all of our meetings and events, including the graduate student panel and year-end graduation ceremony. The graduate student panel alone featured twice as many first-gens as previous meetings had.

Katherine Thomas
BA '16 Kinesiology
Second-year Dental Student
The University of Pennsylvania
School of Dental Medicine

There was a lot of graduate and undergraduate participation across a wide range of disciplines including engineering, business, and medicine. The idea that first-gen graduate students were passing on their knowledge and wanting to help first-gen undergrads further their education speaks to the community that Michigan first-generation students foster as a whole. At the end-of-the-year celebration, we had more graduating seniors participating in our ceremony than ever before.

As a part of our monthly meetings, First-Generation College Students@Michigan became a place to connect and feel comfortable enough to express concerns and struggles facing first-gen students, but the graduation ceremony was different. As the Rogel Ballroom in the Michigan Union filled with graduates and their families, the air was filled with a sense of first-gen joy and pride. It was a time of celebration and self-assurance that we were an innovative group of individuals who possessed the perseverance needed to successfully complete one of the most challenging experiences in life. It was an eye-opening experience and was the first of its kind I had seen during my presidency, as well as in my previous three years at the University of Michigan.

◆

# May

The *Chronicle of Higher Education* publishes an essay by Dwight Lang describing his observations of important and often overlooked first-gen experiences at the University of Michigan: "Singing the First-generation Blues" (May 22, 2015, p. A18–A19). He suggests that "in an era when it's unacceptable to complain about supposed behaviors and attitudes of women and minority-group members, few sanctions exist when working- and lower-class people are belittled. 'First-gen blues' circulate freely at selective colleges like ours." He remarks that he has seen signs in student neighborhoods "inviting revelers to come dressed as trailer trash or ghetto inhabitants. ... Those blues are shaped by three interrelated elements: finances, family and community concerns, and campus culture. ... But those 'first-gen blues' can also be a source of strength as students take risks, persist, meet others from different social-class backgrounds, and cross boundaries to new places where they can realize dreams and accomplishments. Their considerable insights prepare them to live with purpose and become effective professionals, citizens, and parents who have firsthand experiences with class differences." The appearance of this essay in a national higher education publication greatly expands awareness of Michigan's first-gen issues and concerns in Ann Arbor.

# II

## 2015–2016

---

## Fall

"The Rock" at the corner of Hill Street and Washtenaw Avenue is again painted announcing the presence of First-Generation College Students@Michigan. Dwight Lang and Greg Merritt continue as FGCS@M advisers.

Dwight Lang and Greg Merritt

First-gen banner on the Diag

In the summer of 2015, large posters are hung around the Diag welcoming new and continuing first-gen students for the 2015–2016 academic year. Smaller posters highlighting first-gen students and their experiences are strategically placed around campus. Stickers, lapel pins, and other first-gen swag are made available to FGCS@M, student service offices, and interested students. Campus photos are taken to identify individuals involved in FGCS@M efforts. These well-designed efforts to raise awareness of first-gen issues are sponsored and developed by Michigan Creative.

Katie Thomas and Dwight Lang

The November 3, 2015, issue of the *Michigan Daily*, the university's student newspaper, publishes a story featuring FGCS@M students Katie Thomas and Logan Meyer, as well as adviser Dwight Lang: "Faces of Invisible Identity." Katie Thomas describes early months on campus during her first year of college: "If you have parents who went to college, you have some idea of what to expect. I wasn't aware. Everything I came to here was new to me." Logan Meyer also describes key aspects of his first year: "I struggled a lot my first year, especially academically. I hated it. I felt alone. I came here with no one. No one reached out to me, because I looked like every other continuing-gen student." And Dwight Lang summarizes early first-gen experiences at Michigan: "Based on the research, many first-gen students end up being loners because they feel so detached on campuses like this. I've talked to so many first-gens who've seriously thought about leaving even into their sophomore year, because they felt so out of place." This *Michigan Daily* article continues raising awareness of challenging first-gen experiences.

# Winter

The March 2016 issue of the *University Record*, a monthly newspaper for UM Staff and Faculty, reports on a Michigan Creative–sponsored dinner in the Michigan League ballroom celebrating the establishment of a new first generation campus-wide website: "Effort Helps First-Generation Students of U-M Meet Challenges."

# March

*March 9th:* The long-awaited University of Michigan first-generation student website goes live (https://firstgen.studentlife.umich.edu/). This website is institutionally important because significant university funds are used to illustrate first-gen experiences. Many FGCS@M members cannot believe the university has developed this new and needed resource. This dramatically contrasts with the isolation experienced by older Michigan first-gens when they started college. Relevant information, resources, and individuals are identified and continually updated on the website. High school seniors can now read about how the university pays attention to and recognizes first-gen experiences. Current first-gens can also visit the website to check out first-gen campus events and identify useful resources.

With FGCS@M, the Office of the Vice Provost for Diversity, Equity, and Inclusion cosponsors a second winter semester first-gen dinner in the Michigan Union Rogel Ballroom. Vice Provost Rob Sellers again addresses the students and encourages them to be an important part of campus culture. He stresses that first-gens deserve to be at Michigan. Approximately one hundred first-gen students attend. This dinner reflects increasing and continuing institutional support.

# April

The first ever campus-wide Michigan Creative-sponsored First-Gen Symposium is held in the Michigan League. Faculty, staff, and graduate and undergraduate students meet in workshops, at poster sessions, and during panel events to discuss first-generation experiences at the University of Michigan. Dwight Lang's workshop explores how four years at Michigan represents a first-gen portal into the middle

First-gen Symposium

class and upward social mobility experiences. This is not the case for students who grew up in the middle and upper middle classes. Difficult family relationships are discussed as many working-class parents adjust to the fact that their child will live and work in the middle class, perhaps even moving to other parts of the country after graduation. A video program in which current first-gens provide useful advice to new first-gens is presented. One student stresses how the university and first-gens should prioritize the development of personal networks (including peers, staff, and hopefully faculty) that understand first-gen challenges. The primary message of the video is to be open and honest about one's social class background.

Vice Provost for Diversity, Equity, and Inclusion Rob Sellers provides a fourth two-year grant (2016–2018) to support FGCS@M campus activities—the seventh instance of institutional financial support since 2008. Dwight Lang submits the application.

Greg Merritt leaves the University for another employment opportunity but continues to serve as a first-gen adviser, attending some FGCS@M meetings. His considerable insights and contributions to first-gen campus initiatives over the years will be long remembered and appreciated.

The First Generation Student Group continues meeting monthly in the Vice Provost's Office. More staff members in various student service offices are learning about precollege lives of first-gens and the challenges of being in a distinct social class minority on Michigan's campus. Offices implement concrete and useful changes in how they interact with and acknowledge first-gen students, especially during their first year on campus.

Under the Leadership of Professor Sandra Levitsky, the Department of Sociology establishes SOUL: Sociology Opportunities for Undergraduate Leaders. SOUL—the university's first department-level leadership program for first-generation college students—recognizes that first-gens face unique social, academic, and financial challenges. The program provides students with: structured leadership opportunities through UM's Barger Leadership Institute (BLI); a paid Research Assistantship through BLI and the sociology department; a two-credit sociology course exploring the complexities of social mobility; and a first-gen graduate student peer to help navigate the challenges of university culture and evolving nuclear/extended family life. The first SOUL student cohort enrolls for the 2016–2017 academic year. Matthew Sullivan (PhD in sociology '18) is eventually appointed SOUL Director for the 2018–20 academic years.

Students choose a new executive board for the 2016–2017 academic year. Logan Meyer ('17) is elected president.

Another graduation ceremony and dinner, the largest to date, is held in the Michigan Union Rogel Ballroom. Approximately one hundred plus students and their parents celebrate student and family accomplishments.

◆

# Finding Purpose

## Logan Meyer

Logan Meyer
'17 Information Science
Minor: Entrepreneurship
Project Manager, Epic Systems

First-Generation College Students@Michigan was the first place where I found my footing on campus and was the place where I felt Michigan was my home. It was where I learned that I could be successful here and that Michigan wouldn't chew me up and spit me out. Being a part of FGCS@M was one of my greatest campus experiences, and the group helped me launch a pretty amazing college career.

I wanted to become FGCS@M president because I hoped to give back to new first-gen students the feelings of acceptance and hope that it gave me when I was a lost, small-town Michigan freshman. I thought the group's possibilities were fairly close to limitless given how visible and "popular" the first-generation student body had started to become among Michigan's administration and with recruiters from some of the best companies in the world. I saw that wave coming and I really thought our group could take advantage of this newfound awareness. We could launch some great partnerships with other groups on campus, the university itself, and even some of the more elite companies recruiting on our campus.

With those partnerships, I really hoped to create a career fair specifically aimed at first-gens, where companies and graduate schools would talk with students about how to market their unique backgrounds and promote skills they gained from those first-gen experiences in a way that would make them more likely to be hired or accepted into these exclusive programs. FGCS@M members would have a leg up in the competition they often felt left out of due their backgrounds. We were able to do this by putting on an event which pulled first-generation medical, PhD, and law students, as well as professors and professionals from all industries, into a room where our members were then able to question them openly and honestly about their struggles and how they got to where they were in their careers. The most important part was that our members were able to do this without the fear of asking the wrong questions or being judged for not knowing something that a student from a family of college graduates might view as rudimentary knowledge.

FGCS@M was, by far, one of the best things to happen to me during my time at Michigan. I am proud to have been part of such an amazing group and it is still one of my favorite topics to talk about. I hope that future members are able to use what we helped create and that they are able to walk away from FGCS@M with the same benefits it offered to us.

# 12

# 2016–2017

## Fall

Fgcs@M membership grows and students continue reaching out to staff and students; awareness of first-gen experiences expands.

At the late August welcome ceremony for first-year students held in Crisler Arena, Vice Provost for Enrollment Management Kedra Ishop publicly identifies that 12.4 percent of the class of 2020 are first-gen students, up from 10.9 percent five years before. This type of first-gen information has not been part of first-year student welcome events in the past. Once again, first-gen presence is publicly acknowledged by the university. FGCS@M students express pleasant surprise that this type of information is being shared with the public and with continuing generation peers. These first-gen percentages are also reported in the *Ann Arbor News*.

"The Rock" at the corner of Hill Street and Washtenaw Avenue is proudly painted announcing the presence of First Generation College Students@Michigan.

The First Generation Student Group continues meeting monthly in the Vice Provost's Office for Diversity, Equity, and Inclusion.

First-gens, Mason Hall, September 2016

# Winter

Vice Provost for Diversity, Equity, and Inclusion Rob Sellers approves the establishment of a new first-generation student center: the First-Generation Student Gateway. The Gateway will be located in the Office of Academic and Multicultural Initiatives (OAMI), and a full-time project manager, Adan Hussain, is chosen to manage Gateway activities and campus initiatives. This is perhaps the most significant institutional support for Michigan's first-generation students to date. FGCS@M members' and advisers' dedication over the years, as well as support from the administration and the Department of Sociology play major roles in the establishment of this first-generation center. After almost ten years of activism and thoughtful campus engagement, Michigan's first-gen students will finally enjoy a space dedicated to first-gen histories and experiences. Students who had hoped for, worked for, and dreamed of a first-gen center in FGCS@M's earlier years (2008–2016) are remembered.

Students choose a new executive board for the 2017–2018 academic year. Hunter Zhao ('18) is elected president.

Rob Sellers

Ryaan Ooman

Ryann Oomen, a member of the new executive board of FGCS@M, contributes an essay titled "Seeking Stability" to *Social Class Voices: Student Stories from the University of Michigan Bicentennial*, an anthology edited by Dwight Lang and Aubrey Schiavone (Michigan Publishing, 2017). This anthology contains forty-five student essays exploring class experiences in students' families, K–12 education, communities of origin, and undergraduate years. The essays come from a wide range of contributors, whose experiences range from having grown up in poverty and the working clsss to coming from more affluent families.

# April

Another large graduation ceremony and dinner is held in the Michigan Union Rogel Ballroom. Approximately one hundred and twenty students and their parents are present. Susan Dynarski—first-gen and UM Professor of Economics, Education, and Public Policy—gives the keynote address. Susan reflects on her own first-gen experiences as a student and as a faculty member and thanks students for their willingness to champion the first-gen cause.

Susan Dynarski

◆

## *Settling In*

### Hunter Zhao

First-Generation College Students@Michigan seemed like a juggernaut when I served as president (2017–2018). In 2017, everything seemed to align perfectly for Michigan's first-generation community. The university had designated a center specifically for first-generation college students, a full-time staff adviser was appointed to advise students regarding first-generation issues, and corporations and other universities were reaching out to us for advice and professional development opportunities.

Hunter Zhao
BA '18 Sociology and History
Graduate Student, Department of
Human Studies
Columbia University

Yet if you spoke to any member of my former executive board, they would tell you how anxious I felt regarding the success of our organization. Despite the new institutional support and recognition of our community, I feared that FGCS@M would fall apart for the most mundane problem plaguing all student organizations: attendance at bimonthly meetings.

Unlike other student organizations that are goal- or event-oriented—for example, Michigan Active Citizens prepares students to go on alternative spring break trips—FGCS@M is dedicated to providing professional opportunities as well as community building activities for first-gens. This meant that every other week we had to come up with consistently engaging programming that would draw in the first-generation community.

At different points we partnered with Google and with the study abroad office, and we were in conversations with Goldman Sachs. From an administrative perspective, it was difficult to be creative and flexible with the needs of our first-gen community. Missing a week of programming could mean losing the interest of potentially hundreds of first-gen students. Having served on the executive board the previous year, I understood the struggle of attracting students to FGCS@M events and maintaining attendance. At some points there were only ten or so attendees at our meetings.

So, during my presidency, I was adamant not only about building FGCS@M institutionally but also about ensuring that our attendance would mirror at least a fraction of our mailing list, which included more than eight hundred students. Before the first event of the year, we created a plan. In addition to our traditional means of advertising, our executive board would take the time to individually ask other student organizations to invite their first-gens to attend our events. At our first mass meeting, we gave a brief introduction to our organization before handing the event off to a presenter from Google—a very attractive headliner—and we distributed a survey after the event to better understand what our members were looking for from FGCS@M.

And then the day came. The entire floor of the Office of Academic and Multicultural Initiatives (OAMI) was completely filled. It was loud, it was crowded, it was busy, it was exciting, it was hot—it was everything we wanted, and it was nothing we could have imagined. First-gen identity had never felt more salient. The events that followed kept attracting students over and over. At our annual winter semester dinner, we even ran out of food and space because over two hundred students appeared in the first half hour. If I could share anything with future participants in FGCS@M, it would be that this was the year when our organization really took off.

# 13

## 2017–2018

---

## Fall

Professor Karin Martin (also a first-gen) becomes the Department of Sociology Chair in the fall of 2017 and continues departmental support for FGCS@M activities. Also to be recognized are Tamara Kennedy and Nicole Rutherford, sociology major and minor advisers who, over the years, gave budget advice and counsel to the first-gen group as they successfully managed university funds. First-gens are well known for carefully managing their financial resources.

Project Manager for the new First Generation Student Gateway Adan Hussain assumes the role of staff adviser for FGCS@M. During the academic year, FGCS@M transitions from the

Department of Sociology to the Office of Academic and Multicultural Initiatives (OAMI) and the First Generation Student Gateway. Dwight Lang continues as faculty adviser.

The first FGCS@M meeting at the new First Generation Student Gateway, September 2017

The October issue of the *University Record*, Michigan's monthly newspaper for staff and faculty, acknowledges the establishment of the First Generation Student Gateway: "University Dedicates New Space for First-Generation Students." Adan Hussain comments on the new campus initiative: "What we've done is centralized a lot of first-generation efforts. It is really important to us to have a dedicated space because it creates a welcoming area and shows our commitment that we truly want these students here."

The First-Generation Student Group begins monthly meetings

in the Office of Academic and Multicultural Initiatives (OAMI) under the very capable leadership of Adan Hussain.

◆

# A Place to Call Our Own

Adan Hussain

Adan Hussain

I started as First-Generation Project Manager at the University of Michigan in March 2017, after completing my Masters in Higher Education and Student Affairs at The Ohio State University. I report to four different offices: the Office of Academic Multicultural Affairs, the Office of New Student Programs, the Comprehensive Studies Program, and the Multi-Ethnic Student Affairs office.

As a project manager and as a first-generation student myself, I enjoy collaborating with multiple campus units to promote inclusion and success for our first-generation students. My initial charge included the coordination of first-gen related programs, mobilizing campus-wide efforts, improving campus climate for first-generation students, and creating a needed community space that first-generation students could call their own. To that end, I oversee the First-Generation Commission, a campus-wide coalition comprising staff, faculty, and students. Serving as staff adviser for the first-generation student organization, I plan signature programs including the Student–Parent Open House, community dinners, the First-Generation Symposium, and graduation ceremonies for first-generation students and their families.

In October 2017, the Office of Academic Multicultural Initiatives opened the First Generation Gateway, a physical space for first-generation students to connect with resources and build community. I currently work within that Gateway, which now also serves as home base for the decade-old first-generation student organization, First-Generation College Students@Michigan.

◆

## October

First-gen students—once again!—paint "The Rock."

## November–December

Under the leadership of Lauren Schandevel and Meaghan Wheat, first-generation students approach a number of academic departments to discuss the idea

We May Be the First, But We Won't Be the Last

of establishing a new interdisciplinary major: Social Class Studies. Undergraduates would choose courses from a number of academic areas (economics, sociology, psychology, etc.) to examine social class differences and inequalities in America. The Department of Women's Studies agrees to consider a proposal to establish a minor in Social Class Studies. A final decision on establishing this new minor will be made during the 2018–2019 academic year.

# Winter

The *Michigan Daily* student newspaper publishes a story in the January 4, 2018, issue featuring FGCS@M students Wendy Zhuo, Hunter Zhao, and Mia McCrumb, as well as adviser Dwight Lang: "First-Generation Students Discuss Struggles, Opportunities on Campus." Mia McCrumb said her biggest challenge arriving at the University was having no expectations as to what college would be like. ... She says continuing generation students (those whose parents have college degrees) knew what to expect because it was always assumed they would go to college. Hunter Zhao, President of FGCS@M, felt his biggest issues were taking advantage of opportunities offered at the university and with not relating to continuing-generation students from more privileged backgrounds." Wendy Zhuo comments on the second year of college: "As a sophomore, since I've done it once before, I know how the system works now, it's a lot easier. ... Having a community and building connections to people around me helps navigate the whole system." And Dwight Lang advises: "Be proud of who you are: you're a risk-taker and boundary crosser. That's a real strength. ... You might as well be open about it from the get-go." This *Michigan Daily* essay adds to increased awareness of important first-gen experiences at the University of Michigan.

First-gen e-board at winter dinner, Michigan Union

First-gen e-board, 2017-18

The annual first-gen winter dinner is held in the Michigan Student Union. Approximately 200+ students attend, much to the surprise of Adan Hussain, Dwight Lang, and the executive board. New first-gen friendships and networks develop. This is the largest winter semester dinner to date and is a testament to the university's recognition and support of our first-generation students.

Students choose a new executive board for the 2018–2019 academic year. Gabriela "Gaby" Paniagua ('19) is elected president.

First-gen Graduation, Rogel Ballroom, Michigan Union, April 2018

First-gen Graduation, April 2018

## April

The largest graduation ceremony and dinner ever is held in the Michigan Union Rogel Ballroom. Approximately one hundred and thirty graduates and their parents are present. Dwight Lang and Greg Merritt give keynote addresses: Greg Merritt remembers the early years and accomplishments of FGSC@M, and Dwight Lang highlights how words matter and how they should be carefully used to inspire others, protect the least advantaged, build others up, and improve society.

◆

# Fostering First-Gen Empowerment

## Gabriela "Gaby" Paniagua

Gabriela Paniagua
BA '19 Political Science and
Communications
Minor: English

I did not always understand what it meant to be a first-generation student. When I initially joined the first-gen organization, it allowed me to better understand my own identity and embrace who I was—who I am. I became a member after going to various campus events, and taking everything in was an eye-opening experience. But I wanted more. I wanted to be on the executive board and drive some of the discussions that were happening. So that is exactly what I did.

Now, as President of First-Generation Students@Michigan, I have many goals and visions for our organization. I am excited about the coming year and I'm hopeful that we will remain strong for years to come. We can have a bigger presence on campus, allowing first-generation students to find and participate in the group sooner rather than later. The ultimate goal of the organization is to create a community and space for first-gens to feel supported and empowered. We also want to inform students about campus resources so they do not have to struggle to find them. For first-gens, college is full of many firsts, and for me, being president is also a first. Although it is a bit scary having this leadership role, I am confident that together with the executive board, our mentors, and other partners, we will be able to make the organization a great success for another year.

The first-generation group has been around for ten years, and it always warms me to hear the story of how it started years ago with some meetings in the home of Dwight and Sylvia Lang, instead of a campus classroom space. Years later the organization has come a long way. We are now based in the Office of Academic Multi-cultural Initiatives under the mentorship of Adan Hussain. I am thankful for all the resources OAMI and Adan have provided us. I am honored to be the new president of First-Generation College Students@Michigan, and I am confident that we will be able to break through new barriers.

# 14

# 2018–2019

---

## September

The September 28 edition of the *Chronicle of Higher Education* publishes an essay by Dwight Lang describing challenges of first-generation upward social mobility on college campuses—like Michigan—where the vast majority of undergraduates have grown up in economic privilege: "Social Mobility Comes at a Cost" (pp. B22, B24; see essay graphic). He comments: "Students from disadvantaged backgrounds attend highly selective colleges with great expectations. But because their families may value group needs over individual aspirations, campus traditions of middle-class individualism and competition can feel alien. Most working-class students, who are typically first in their families to attend college and often from rural areas, haven't lived outside their communities before. They're understandably cautious when interacting with peers from comfortable, suburban areas." This essay, featured in a nationwide higher education publication, helps expand readers' understanding of Michigan's first-gen issues and concerns.

From Dwight Lang's *Chronicle of Higher Education* essay, 9/18/18. Used with permission of the artist, Jack Molloy.

# October

The Department of Women's Studies—under the the leadership of Professor Abby Stewart—approves the establishment of a new minor: Social Class and Inequality Studies. The proposal is sent to the Curriculum Committee in the College of Literature, Science, and Arts for further consideration.

# November

The First-Generation Symposium is held once again. Michigan's faculty and staff meet to examine best practices in supporting first-generation students. The symposium engages the campus in valuable dialogue around helping first-generation students to thrive and not merely survive. Dwight Lang leads a session examining challenges faced by first-generation students on campuses like the University of Michigan where middle and upper middle class students are in the majority. The symposium examines four important aspects: 1) understanding first generation students and their intersecting identities; 2) teaching and advising; 3) data and evaluation; 4) assessment, admission, retention, and graduate success. This second first-gen symposium represents an increasing university commitment to promoting successful social class diversity.

# December

National Public Radio posts a story: "'Going to Office Hours Is Terrifying' and Other Tales of Rural Students in College" (December 12, 2018). The essay reviews experiences of a number of first-gen students from rural areas attending the University of Michigan. They are acutely aware of social class divides in Ann Arbor, where the median family income is $156,000—three times the state of Michigan's average. One student comments: "Everybody has got the coin that I don't have. Those Canada Goose jackets? You've got to be kidding." (Many students wear Canada Goose–brand jackets, which sell for as much as $1,550 each.) "I'm walking down the road and I see people with Gucci or Versace."

Interviewed first-gens don't always feel comfortable, but the essay clarifies how the university publicly recognizes student negotiations of sometimes difficult college social class experiences and adjustments.

# January

The Curriculum Committee of the College of Literature, Science, and Arts formally approves the Inequality and Social Class Studies minor. Students will begin enrolling for the fall semester of 2019. This is the first academic program in the nation to examine how social class is structured and experienced.

The university establishes the First Generation and Low Income Student Support Taskforce. First-gen students are asked to be members. Adan Hussain and Dwight Lang are invited to participate. Taskforce purposes are to: 1) examine social class diversity at the University of Michigan; 2) consider how the university can improve support for first-generation students; 3) explore how the university can provide a stronger sense of belonging for first-gen students; 4) identify best practices for serving first-gen and low income students. A final report will be completed by the end of June and delivered to Vice Provosts Kendra Ishop (Enrollment Management), Robert Sellers (Office of Diversity, Equity, and Inclusion), Amy Dittmar (Academic and Budgetary Affairs), as well as Vice President E. Royster Harper (Student Life).

# April

E-board elections are held. Anita Ho is elected president for 2019-2020.

Plans are made for the annual first-generation graduation on April 29 in the Michigan League Ballroom. By early April 216 students have RSVP's. This will surpass the 2018 graduation in the Rogel Ballroom of the Michigan Union when a record 130 students and their parents attended. This anticipated 600+ first-gen graduation ceremony surpasses the first, first-gen end of the year celebration in 2008 when five first-gens (the founding-five) and three advisers gathered in the third floor, Michigan Union pool hall. "We may be the first, but we won't be the last."

First Gens Skating at Yost Arena: February 2019

First-gen E-Board, 2019-20

Students/Parents arriving at 2019 First-gen graduation, Michigan League Ballroom

First-gen Graduation 2019 cookie

Dwight Lang, 2019 First-gen graduation, Michigan League

# Coda

## Winter Semester 2019

First-Generation College Students@Michigan completes twelve years of active presence at the University of Michigan in Ann Arbor to *recognize, raise awareness of, and resolve* first-generation student concerns and issues.

Without the active, consistent, and energetic participation of dozens of first-generation Michigan undergraduates over a dozen years, First-Generation College Students@Michigan would not have continued to be an active force for needed change. Student, adviser, staff, administrator, and faculty contributions and support identified in this brief history will always be remembered by past, present, and future first-gens who will continue to proclaim: "We may be the first, but we won't be the last." And as always: *Go Blue!*

# Appendix: Agreement of Sponsorship

2008-2009

**Agreement of Sponsorship**

**of First-Generation College Students @ Michigan**

**by the Department of Sociology**

This document is an agreement between the Department of Sociology (Sociology) and First-Generation College Students @ Michigan (FGS@M), a student organization recognized by the Michigan Student Assembly. The agreement 1) describes the purposes of a sponsorship agreement, 2) details the provisions of the agreement, and 3) describes the primary responsibilities of each party.

**Purpose of sponsorship**

Sponsored status for a student organization is a statement of recognition by the University of Michigan that student organizations are key elements in helping the University realize its mission as well the department's mission. The sponsoring relationship encourages University academic departments and student affairs units to support the potential of student organizations to actively contribute to the cultural, social, and academic life on campus, making the Michigan experience meaningful. The sponsoring department views the organization, through its efforts, as worthwhile and vital, and therefore commits itself to provide support for the organization and its goals.

**Provisions of the sponsorship agreement**

I.     Sociology recognizes the importance of the FGS@M's self-direction and student leadership in the development of productive campus stewards and alumni. However, a sponsored student organization is a representative of the University, and the Sociology requires a high level of accountability from FGS@M.

II.    Sociology will offer FGS@M the following resources in order facilitate recognition of first-generation college students on Michigan's campus and resolve any needs that are uncovered in that recognition and awareness-raising:

- Office space in 3147 LSA Building. This office will be shared with the Undergraduate Sociology Association.

- A dedicated staff advisor, the department's undergraduate program director, who will act as a liaison between Sociology's administrative leaders and FGS@M, and provide leadership counseling. If an irreconcilable conflict between the advisor and FGS@M

Page 1 of 4

116

arises, Sociology's chair and administrative manager will mediate the conflict and facilitate a resolution.

- Mailing address (3147 LSA Building, 500 S. State Street, Ann Arbor, MI 48109-1382)

- Reasonable use of the department's photocopier, a reasonable amount of a paper for fliers and meeting materials, paper plates, cups, and napkins for events, and other limited office supplies as requested and approved by the advisor and department manager.

- Direct financial allocation of $100.00 each fall and winter semester to FGS@M.

III. Sociology and FGS@M recognize the important role of the Standards of Conduct for Recognized Student Organizations in the student organization accountability process. FGS@M agrees to abide by these standards found at www.studentorgs.umich.edu/download/StandardsofConduct-5-8-07.pdf.

IV. The Department of Sociology and the First-Generation College Students @ Michigan will meet on December 3, 2008 to negotiate and sign this agreement. This sponsorship agreement is expected to be submitted to the Office of Student Activities and Leadership on December 4, 2008.

V. FGS@M will not enter into University or non-University contracts, or risk being held personally liable for contractual obligations. When entering into a contract becomes a requirement for a group's activities, the group will seek advice from the designated advisor.

VI. FGS@M will be able to accept to tax deductible gifts through Sociology's financial structure and will abide by the procedures established by Sociology's financial specialist.

VII. Although the Office of Student Activities and Leadership automatically renews sponsorship agreements each year, FGS@M and Sociology will review and sign the agreement each year. Either party may initiate a modification to the agreement by communicating the intended modification to the group's advisor, who will facilitate a negotiation between the department's administrators and FGS@M. In the event of a new department chair or new undergraduate program coordinator, a new agreement will be negotiated, signed, and submitted.

2008-2009

All parties named below agree with the terms of this sponsorship agreement.

Howard Kimeldorf, Chair, Department of Sociology

Jennifer Eshelman, Department Manager, Department of Sociology

Elise Frankish, Undergraduate Program Coordinator, Department of Sociology; FG@M advisor

Aimee Von Bokel

Chyrisha Brown

Alexa DiFiore

Cimrie Ream

Carley J. Flanery

Lauren Sterrett

Sara Pikora

2008-2009

Candyce Hill

KRISTIN Lo

Dwight Lang

December 3, 2008

# About the Author

*Dwight Lang* is Lecturer in the Department of Sociology at the University of Michigan, Ann Arbor and Professor Emeritus at Madonna University, in Livonia, Michigan. Since 2008 he has been Faculty Adviser to First Generation College Students@Michigan, an undergraduate group for students who are first in their families to attend college. He was first in his family to attend college. His publications include: *Social Class Voices: Student Stories from the University of Michigan Bicentennial*, Michigan Publishing, 2017 (edited with Aubrey Schiavone); "The Social Construction of a Working Class Academic," in *This Fine Place So Far From Home: Voices of Academics from the Working Class*, C. L. Barney Dews and Carolyn Leste Law (eds), Temple University Press, 1995; "Those of Us from Rio Linda," in *Class Lives: Stories from Across Our Economic Divide*, Chuck Collins, et. al. (eds), Cornell University Press, 2014; "Social Mobility Comes at a Cost," *The Chronicle of Higher Education: Diversity in Academe*, September 28, 2018, P. B22/

24; "Singing the First-Generation Blues," *The Chronicle of Higher Education: Diversity in Academe,* Volume LXI, Number 36, May 22, 2015, P. A18-A19; and "Witnessing Social Class in the Academy," in *Working in Class: Recognizing How Social Class Shapes Our Academic Work,* Allison Hurst and Sandi Kawecka (eds), Rowman & Littlefield, 2016.